CASPiAN

Biomes
of North
America

A Walk
in the
Rain
Forest

by Rebecca L. Johnson

with illustrations by Phyllis V. Saroff

CAROLRHODA BOOKS, INC./MINNEAPOLIS

For my niece Claire, who helps me see
the world with fresh eyes
—R. L. J.

Text copyright © 2001 by Rebecca L. Johnson
Illustrations copyright © 2001 by Phyllis V. Saroff

Map on page 8 by Laura Westlund © 2001 by Carolrhoda Books, Inc.

Carolrhoda Books, Inc.
A division of Lerner Publishing Group
241 First Avenue North
Minneapolis, Minnesota 55401 U.S.A.

Website address: www.lernerbooks.com

Library of Congress Cataloging-in-Publication Data

Johnson, Rebecca L.
  A walk in the rain forest / by Rebecca L. Johnson ; illustrations by
Phyllis V. Saroff.
    p.   cm. — (Biomes of North America)
  Includes index.
  Summary: Takes readers on a walk through a tropical rain forest,
showing examples of how the animals and plants depend on each other
and their environment to survive.
  ISBN 1-57505-154-0 (lib. bdg. : alk. paper)
1. Rain forest ecology—Juvenile literature. 2. Rain forests—
Juvenile literature. [1. Rain forest ecology. 2. Rain forests.
3. Ecology.] I. Saroff, Phyllis V., ill. II. Title. III. Series: Johnson,
Rebecca L. Biomes of North America.
QH541.5.R27 J66 2001
577.34—dc21   00-008244

Manufactured in the United States of America
2 3 4 5 6 7 - JR - 06 05 04 03 02 01

Words
to Know

ALGAE (AL-jee)—plantlike living things

BIOME (BYE-ohm)— a major community of living things that covers a large area, such as a grassland or forest

BROMELIADS (broh-MEE-lee-adz)— plants with spiky leaves that overlap in the center to form a cup

BUTTRESSES (BUT-truh-sez)— triangular-shaped plates of wood that flare out from the bottoms of some rain forest tree trunks

CANOPY (KAN-uh-pee)—the "roof" of the rain forest, made up of the tops of the tallest trees

CLIMATE (KLYE-mut)—a region's usual pattern of weather over a long period of time

DISGUISE (dis-GIZE)—something that hides a living thing's true identity

EPIPHYTE (EH-puh-fite)—a plant that grows on another plant

FUNGI (FUHN-gye)—living things such as mushrooms or molds that get their food by breaking down dead plant and animal matter

LIANAS (lee-AH-nuhz)—woody vines

NECTAR—a sweet liquid made by flowers. Nectar is used as food by animals such as bats, bees, and hummingbirds.

PREDATORS (PREH-duh-turz)—animals that hunt and eat other animals

PREHENSILE (pree-HEN-suhl)—able to wrap around and grab onto something

PREY (pray)—animals that are hunted and eaten by other animals

TROPICAL (TRAH-pih-kuhl)—a place near the equator that is hot and humid

UNDERSTORY—a layer of smaller trees and bushes below the canopy of taller trees in a rain forest

Hot, humid, and incredibly green

Towering trees line the banks of a narrow river. They form dark green walls on either side of the muddy water. Insects buzz and hum. The bright sun is hot. The air feels sticky. A howler monkey sits on a branch that hangs over the river. Below him, two bulging eyes and a long snout bob to the surface. It's a crocodile.

Tipping back his head, the monkey howls. *Aaaarrrrooooo-ooo-oooo-gaaahhhh!* His howl warns of danger here in the tropical rain forest.

Tropical rain forests are steamy, shadowy, and packed with living things.

The rain forest is full of strange shadows, smells, and sounds. It is warm and wet and incredibly green. A dense tangle of trees and other plants fills every space. Hidden among all the leaves and branches are all sorts of animals. Tropical rain forests overflow with life.

Where can you find tropical rain forests? Near the equator, where it is always warm and it rains nearly every day. The largest rain forests are in South America, Africa, and Asia. In North America, rain forests stretch from Mexico to Panama. Some Caribbean islands are covered by rain forests, too.

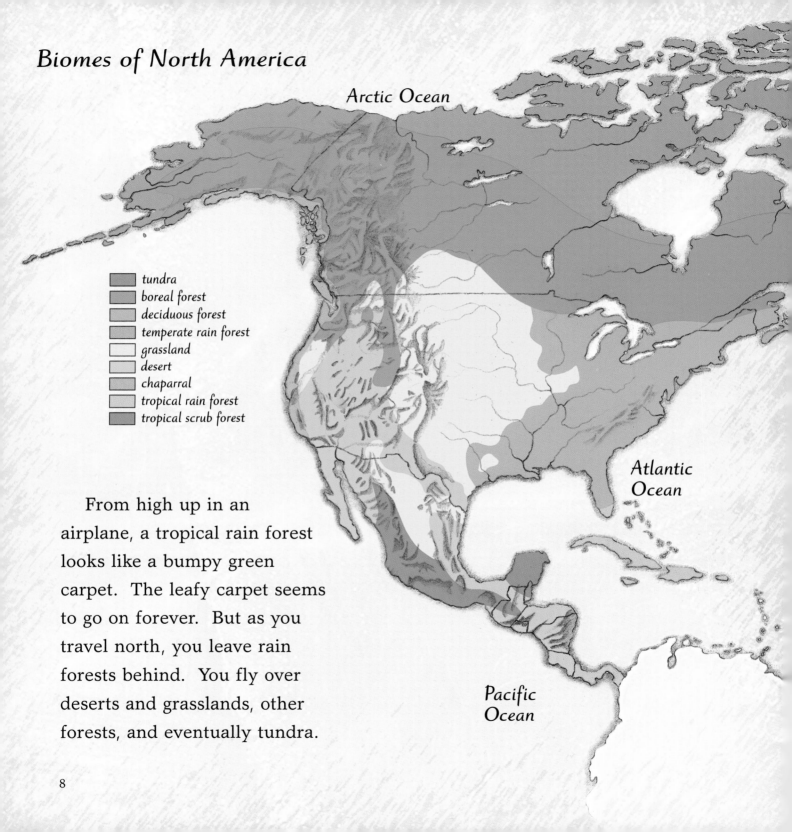

Biomes of North America

Arctic Ocean

Atlantic Ocean

Pacific Ocean

- tundra
- boreal forest
- deciduous forest
- temperate rain forest
- grassland
- desert
- chaparral
- tropical rain forest
- tropical scrub forest

From high up in an airplane, a tropical rain forest looks like a bumpy green carpet. The leafy carpet seems to go on forever. But as you travel north, you leave rain forests behind. You fly over deserts and grasslands, other forests, and eventually tundra.

Forests, grasslands, deserts, and tundra make up
Earth's main land zones. Scientists call these zones
biomes.

Each biome has a different type of climate. The
climate is an area's usual pattern of weather over a
long period of time.

Every biome is home to a special group of plants.
The plants are well suited to living in that biome's
climate and to growing in the soil found there.

Every biome is also home to a special group of
animals. In one way or another, the animals depend
on the plants to survive. Many of a biome's animals
eat plants. Others eat the plant-eaters.

*Sun shines through
falling rain, and a
rainbow arches over
the crowded tops of
rain forest trees.*

Orchids are beautiful flowers that thrive in a rain forest climate.

Bathed in mist, leafy green plants grow in every available bit of space (above right).

All the plants and animals in a biome form a community. In that community, every living thing depends on other community members for its survival. A biome's climate, soil, plants, and animals are all connected this way.

The tropical rain forest has a warm, wet climate. From day to day, and month to month, the temperature changes very little. It rains almost every day. Even when it's not raining, the rain forest is dripping and damp.

A hummingbird sips sweet nectar from a tropical flower.

With all that water and warmth, rain forest plants grow nonstop. Whether it's July or January, the rain forest is always leafy and green. Thousands of different kinds of plants provide food and shelter for millions of animals. Rain forests are home to more than half of all the types of plants and animals that live on Earth.

A mushroom makes a comfy chair for a tiny poison dart frog (above left).

11

Along the riverbank, close to where the crocodile appeared, there's a small opening in the trees. Let's enter and take a walk in the rain forest.

Push aside the tangled vines and step into a world of green shadows. The air is warm, humid, and still. There isn't even a whisper of a breeze. Except for a few birdcalls and the hum of insects, it's very quiet. The ground is covered with a thin layer of dead leaves. Push aside a few leaves. You'll find sticky red-brown mud. It smells like moldy clay.

There is just enough room to walk between the tree trunks and the tangle of twisting vines.

Wait for your eyes to get used to the dim light. All around you, the trunks of huge trees rise straight up. High overhead, the trees branch out into broad, leafy tops. The treetops form a canopy. Like an enormous green umbrella, the canopy covers the rain forest. It is so thick it blocks out the sky.

Sunbeams filter down through the canopy. Plants use sunlight to make their own food.

Clinging vines hold tight to other plants as they grow up toward the light.

Sturdy buttresses grow out in all directions from the base of a huge tree.

Many trees have buttresses. Buttresses are plates of very hard wood that flare out from the bottoms of the trunks. Woody vines called lianas twist around the tree trunks. Lianas grow up, up, up, until they disappear in the canopy of leaves.

A vine called a strangler fig coils around a tree trunk. Eventually, the strangler fig will kill the tree.

Some lianas are thicker than your leg.

The densely packed rain forest has three main layers: canopy, understory, and forest floor. Some trees are so tall that they emerge from the canopy.

Broad leaves of a banana plant surround a cluster of small sweet bananas.

Beneath the canopy is the understory of smaller trees and bushes. Only a little sunlight filters through the canopy and understory to the ground. The plants that grow on the shadowy forest floor have very large leaves to catch as much light as they can. Plants need sunlight to grow.

But where are all the animals? Some are hiding in
the shadows nearby. Many others live high above
you. They rarely, if ever, come down to the ground.

*A squirrel monkey
looks out over the
forest from its perch
high in the trees.*

How can you see them? Rain forest researchers
often build platforms in the canopy. They use ropes
to move up and down through the trees. There's a
platform far overhead. See the ropes hanging down?
Let's go up for a better look.

Climb through the tangled vines and branches of the understory. You're 40, 80, 100 feet up. It's getting lighter. Now you're 120 feet above the ground—higher than a 10-story building. A few more feet, and bright sun makes you squint. You've reached the canopy. You're on the roof of the rain forest.

Airy and bright, the canopy stretches out for miles and miles.

Billions of shiny leaves rustle in the breeze. The air is full of sweet smells. Some of the trees around you are blooming. Covered with flowers, they are islands of color in a sea of green. Their bright flowers attract bees and wasps. A butterfly swoops past. Its blue wings glint like metal in the sun.

Tropical rain forests are home to the largest and most unusual butterflies in the world.

A blue morpho butterfly suns itself on a leaf.

A long-tailed hermit hummingbird hovers in midair while it sips nectar from a ginger flower. Hummingbirds can beat their wings one hundred times a second.

Hummingbirds visit the flowers, too. Like tiny helicopters, they hover in front of the blossoms. With their long, slender bills, they reach the sweet nectar inside.

Other trees have finished flowering. Their branches are covered with seedpods or fleshy fruit. Some seedpods explode when they are ripe, hurling out their seeds. Other pods have seeds with papery wings or fluffy tops. The wind may carry these seeds great distances.

Many rain forest fruits are eaten by animals.
The seeds inside the fruit end up in the animals'
droppings. As animals move from place to place,
they scatter the seeds far and wide.

Cashews ripen in the sun (below).
A scarlet macaw dines on a
papaya (right).

With two toes in front and two toes in back, a macaw's foot can grip like a clamp.

Not far from you, a dozen toucans are eating figs. They pluck the fruits with their huge rainbow-colored beaks. Then they tilt back their heads and swallow the figs whole.

A pair of scarlet macaws flies in to join the feast. Screeching and squawking, the big birds hang upside down to reach the ripest figs.

A keel-billed toucan holds a nut in its extraordinary beak.

A prehensile tail can wrap around a branch and hold on tight.

Fruit is a favorite food of monkeys, too. Furry black howlers, graceful capuchins, and long-limbed spider monkeys are the acrobats of the canopy. They swing from branch to branch, holding on with hands and feet and the tips of their prehensile tails. A prehensile tail can curl around and hold on to things. It's like having an extra hand.

Hanging on with its tail, a white-fronted capuchin uses both hands to tear apart a fruit (above left).

23

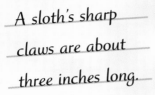

A sloth's sharp claws are about three inches long.

Hanging upside down, a mother sloth cradles her baby against her furry chest (above right).

In the top of another tree, you spot what looks like a bunch of leaves. But this green clump has a smiling face! It's a sloth. Sloths hang upside down by their long, hooklike claws. They move very, very slowly.

A sloth's fur looks green because tiny green algae grow on it. A small moth called a sloth moth also lives in sloth fur. Sloth moth caterpillars eat the algae on the fur.

Wherever you look in a rain forest, there is life of some kind. Something is growing or hiding or resting in every tiny space. Tree branches, too, are crowded with life. They are covered with epiphytes. Epiphytes are plants that grow on other plants.

A sloth moth lays her eggs in a sloth's thick fur.

Epiphytes crowd together on a tree's thick branches.

Tiny bromeliad ponds attract all sorts of animals.

Raindrops shimmer on the waxy petals of an orchid.

Orchids are epiphytes that have delicate, strange-looking flowers. Bromeliads are epiphytes, too. Their long, spiky leaves overlap in the center to form a cup. The cup holds a tiny pond of rainwater. Snails and beetles live in these bromeliad ponds. Some frogs lay their eggs in them. Birds and monkeys use them as drinking fountains.

Rain collects in the center
of a bromeliad (right).

A bromeliad begins to flower (above).
Searching for a bromeliad pond,
a strawberry poison dart frog carries its
tadpole piggyback (right).

Leaves with pointed "drip-tips" shed rainwater quickly.

Mist rises from the treetops as a sudden rain drenches the canopy.

Clouds have gathered over the forest. Lightning flashes. Thunder rumbles. Raindrops begin to fall. The leaves of most rain forest plants are thick and waxy. They come to a point called a drip-tip. When it rains, water runs down to the tip and quickly drips off.

It's raining harder. Water is dripping off leaves and trickling down branches. Monkeys and birds take cover under big leaves. But the sloth doesn't seem to mind getting wet. Its shaggy fur grows from its belly toward its back, so rainwater runs off as the sloth hangs upside down.

Ignoring the rain, a sloth creeps along a branch toward a cluster of tasty leaves.

The understory is so dense that there's hardly room to move.

Climb down below the treetops. The canopy blocks most of the rain. There's just a steady drip, drip, drip as water moves from leaf to leaf on its way down through the forest.

Take a rest 50 feet above the ground. Here in the understory, there is much less room to move around. Lianas zigzag from branch to branch like tangled bunches of rope.

Most trees flower from buds at the end of their leafy twigs. But the flowers of many understory trees sprout directly from a branch or a trunk. Without lots of leaves in the way, it's easier for bees to find the flowers.

Big sturdy flowers grow straight out of the cannonball tree's trunk. The flowers turn into large, hard-shelled fruits that look like cannonballs.

The plump seedpods of a cacao tree grow right out of its trunk. Cacao seeds are used to make chocolate.

When the fruits of the cannonball tree are ripe, they drop off and crash down onto the forest floor.

Slim as a pencil, a vine
snake slithers among
the leaves (left).

Long toes and sharp
claws give an iguana
(right) a good grip as it
scrambles up and down
through the understory
trees.

A poison dart frog (left) clings to a slippery leaf using sticky pads on the tips of its toes. Large eyes help a red-eyed tree frog (above) see well in the dim light of the understory.

Do you feel like you're being watched? You probably are. The animals of the understory are all around. Tree snakes twine among the branches and vines. Sharp-clawed iguanas rest on thick trunks. Tree frogs use their round, sticky toes to cling to slippery stems. A few kinds of frogs are transparent. Others are dull brown or vivid green. But the deadly poison dart frogs are crayon-bright colors of orange, blue, yellow, and red.

Birds are hard to see in the dense understory. But you can hear them call to each other. There's the ringing cry of the bellbird. It's so loud and clear it can be heard more than a mile away. Listen for the manakin's curious clicks and the low booming notes of a curassow. The strange cry of *cha-cha-la-ca* belongs to the chachalaca. Its name sounds just like its song.

Some insects that live in the understory look like sticks, dead leaves, or flower petals. These disguises usually fool insect-eating birds. Other insects have stripes and spots that make them hard to see.

The resplendent quetzal is one of the most beautiful birds in the rain forest.

Some tropical treehoppers look like sharp thorns on a plant's stem.

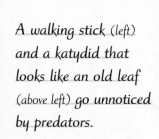

A walking stick (left) and a katydid that looks like an old leaf (above left) go unnoticed by predators.

Nothing stops army ants as they march through the forest. Soldier army ants have huge jaws. They are bigger than worker army ants.

On the march—army ants swarm across the ground (right). Azteca ants (below) are quick to defend their cecropia tree home.

If there's one kind of animal you're sure to see here, it's ants. There are green ants, brown ants, and black ants. There are big ants with scary jaws. And there are tiny ants hardly bigger than a speck of dirt.

Some rain forest ants live only on certain plants. Azteca ants live on cecropia trees. The ants and the trees help each other to survive. Cecropia trees provide the ants with food and a safe place to live. The ants bite and sting animals that try to eat cecropia leaves. They bump off epiphyte seeds that land on the branches. They snip the tendrils of clinging vines.

Can you imagine eating ants? That's what the tamandua does. With its long, sticky tongue, the tamandua laps up ants as it climbs through the understory.

Long claws and a prehensile tail help a tamandua climb trees in search of ants.

A tamandua sniffs out ants using its keen sense of smell.

A land crab waves its big front claw as a warning (left). The damp forest floor (below) is alive with creatures that scurry, slither, and creep.

A deadly fer-de-lance coils on the forest floor, ready to strike.

Climb all the way back down to the forest floor. Fallen branches, rotting fruit, and dead leaves lie scattered at your feet. Crabs, scorpions, and slugs creep through all this litter. You see centipedes as long as pencils, and furry-legged tarantulas, the largest spiders in the world. Boa constrictors and coral snakes may be hiding here, too. Watch your step!

Slowly and silently, a boa constrictor moves into the light (above left).

39

Mushrooms sprout from fallen logs. Cottony strands of fungus cling to rotting leaves. Ants and worms and even tinier creatures break the forest's wastes into smaller pieces. They turn it into soil that feeds the plants and helps them to grow.

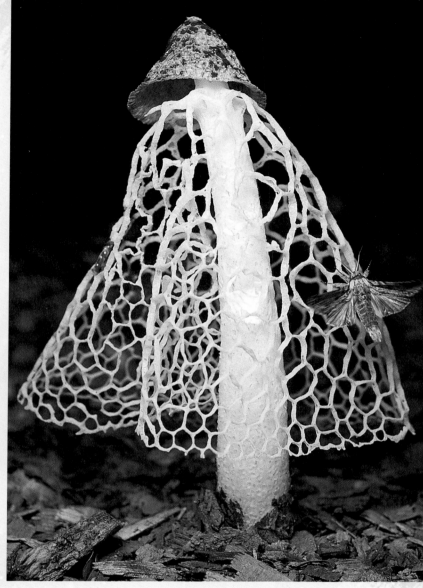

Dainty mushrooms sprout from a rotting log (left). The bridal veil stinkhorn fungus (above) is beautiful, but it gives off a terrible smell. This moth doesn't seem to mind.

A line of leaf-cutter ants moves across the forest floor (above). In their underground nest, the ants eat the fungus that grows on chewed-up leaves (left).

Leaf-cutter ants carry neatly snipped bits of leaves.

At your feet, bits of green leaves seem to be moving across the ground all by themselves. Look closer. The leaves are carried by leaf-cutter ants. With scissorlike jaws, the ants cut up leaves and carry them to underground nests. There, a pale fungus grows on the leafy bits. The ants eat the fungus as their food.

41

A family of white-lipped peccaries searches for fallen fruit on the forest floor.

As you walk back toward the river, a white-lipped peccary snorts in surprise. It scoots away into the shadows. Peccaries are piglike animals. They eat roots and leaves and fallen fruit.

Peccaries try to avoid jaguars, the largest predators in the rain forest. Jaguars often stretch out on tree branches. When an animal like a peccary walks by, the jaguar silently drops down. Luckily for you, jaguars hunt mostly at night.

Lurking in the shadows, a jaguar silently stalks its prey.

43

Like a shadow dropping from the night sky, a bat swoops down on a frog.

Safe in the treetops, a capuchin relaxes as the sun begins to set. At sunrise, he'll be on the move again.

It has been a long day. The sun is setting. High in the trees, owls and bats are waking up. Other night hunters, like the jaguars, will soon be on the prowl. As darkness deepens, fireflies flash like twinkling stars.

Thousands of tree frogs are singing. Their noisy chorus of chirps and peeps will last all through the night.

Overhead, capuchins and howler monkeys are curled up in the branches. They are quiet and ready for sleep. But at dawn, the monkeys will howl again as another day in the rain forest begins.

From their perch in the canopy, two toucans watch night descend on the rain forest.

for further
Information
about the Rain Forest

Books

Banks, Joan. *Song of La Selva: A Story of a Costa Rican Rain Forest.* Norwalk, CT: Soundprints, 1998.

Chinery, Michael. *Rainforest Animals.* New York: Random House, 1992.

Cowcher, Helen. *Jaguar.* New York: Scholastic, 1997.

Forsyth, Adrian. *How Monkeys Make Chocolate: Foods and Medicines from the Rainforests.* New York: Firefly, 1995.

Fredericks, Anthony. *Slugs.* Minneapolis: Lerner, 2000.

George, Jean Craighead. *One Day in the Tropical Rainforest.* New York: Harper, 1995.

Julivert, Angels. *The Fascinating World of Ants.* Hauppauge, NY: Barron's, 1991.

Kalman, Bobbie. *Rainforest Birds.* New York: Crabtree, 1998.

Lasky, Kathryn. *The Most Beautiful Roof in the World: Exploring the Rain Forest Canopy.* San Diego: Harcourt Brace, 1997.

Netherton, John. *Red-Eyed Tree Frogs.* Minneapolis: Lerner, 2001.

Souza, D. M. *Roaring Reptiles.* Minneapolis: Carolrhoda, 1992.

Squire, Ann O. *Anteaters, Sloths, and Armadillos.* New York: Franklin Watts, 1999.

Storad, Conrad J. *Tarantulas.* Minneapolis: Lerner, 1998.

Swan, Erin Pembrey. *Primates: From Howler Monkey to Humans.* New York: Franklin Watts, 1998.

Yolen, Jane. *Welcome to the Green House.* New York: Putnam, 1993.

Websites

Animals of the Rain Forest
< http://animalsoftherainforest.org >

Developed by a sixth grade class, this site offers facts and photographs of the animals of the rain forest.

Central America's National Parks
< http://www.nps.gov/centralamerica/ >

The National Park Service offers a guide to national parks of Central America. Follow the link for "A Sample of Diversity," then click on the country of your choice to learn about the rain forests of Central America.

Rainforest Action Network Kids' Corner
< http://www.ran.org/kids_action/index1
.html >

Learn about threats to the rain forest and what you can do to stop them. This site also provides information about people who live in the rain forest and rain forest wildlife.

Rainforest Alliance—For Kids and Teachers
< http://www.rainforestalliance.org
/kids&teachers/ >

This site features information about rain forest frogs, along with activities and artwork. It also provides ideas to help kids save the rain forest.

Rainforest Biome
< http://mbgnet.mobot.org/sets/rforest
/index.htm >

This site from the Evergreen Project features general information about rain forests. Follow a student along on a trip to the rain forest around Tikal, Guatemala.

*A Sampling of Tropical Rainforest
 Animals*
< http://www.allaboutnature.com
/subjects/rainforest/animals
/Rfbiomeanimals.shtml >

This site offers a guide to the rain forest and its animal life.

Photo Acknowledgments

The images in this book are used with the permission of: © Carrol Henderson, pp. 4-5, 29, 35 (bottom), 36 (bottom), 45; © Kevin Schafer, pp. 5, 9, 10, 17, 20, 21 (right), 23, 24, 25, 26, 27 (top right), 31, 32 (right), 33 (right), 34, 35 (top), 36 (top), 37, 40 (right), 42, 44; © Gary Braasch Photography, pp. 6-7, 13, 15, 21 (left), 28, 30, 33 (left), 38 (bottom), 39; © Tom Boyden, pp. 11, 12, 14, 16, 18-19, 19 (bottom), 22, 32 (left), 41 (top and bottom), 43; © André Bärtschi, pp. 27 (left and bottom right), 38 (top), 40 (left).

Front cover: © André Bärtschi (iguana), © Gary Braasch Photography (macaws, background).

Index

Numbers in **bold** refer to photos and drawings.